THE ART OF BEING YOU

A JOURNEY OF SELF LOVE AND FORGIVING OTHERS

ARPIT SADH

Made with ♥ on the Notion Press Platform
www.notionpress.com

For the dreamers and the doubters, the seekers and the silent fighters.

Contents

Introduction

Why Being You is an Art

Who Are You When No One Is Watching?

Picture this: It's late at night. The world has quieted down. You're lying in bed, staring at the ceiling, scrolling through your phone, or maybe just sitting in silence with your own thoughts.

And then, like clockwork, it happens.

That tiny, nagging voice creeps in the one that whispers:

"Am I doing life right?"

"Why does everyone else seem happier?"

"Will I ever feel like enough?"

In a world that constantly tells us who to be successful, lovable, perfect it's easy to lose sight of the most important thing: **being yourself.** But let's face it, being you in today's world can feel like the hardest thing to do.

We live in an age where loneliness feels like an epidemic despite being hyperconnected. Relationships can feel shallow, heartbreak stings deeper than ever, and procrastination and laziness creep in, paralyzing us from achieving our goals. Sound familiar? You're not alone.

But here's the thing: the art of being you isn't about fixing yourself. It's about rediscovering the beauty of who you already are, flaws and all. It's about forgiving the people who've hurt you—not because they deserve it, but because you do. And most importantly, it's about learning to forgive yourself for all the times you didn't meet your own expectations.

This book is a conversation between you and me. Think of it as a friend who sits down with you on a quiet evening and says, ***"Hey, let's figure this out together."*** You'll learn to embrace solitude without feeling lonely, heal from heartbreak without losing hope, and conquer procrastination without self-judgment.

By the time you turn the last page, you'll realize that the art of being you is less about becoming someone new and more about coming home to yourself. And isn't that what we all crave a home within ourselves where we are truly at peace?

Let's begin.

The Journey To Self Love

CHAPTER I

The Mask We Wear

Who Do You Pretend to Be?

Have you ever felt like you're living someone else's life? *Like you're playing a role in a movie that you never auditioned for?* Let's be honest, we've all worn masks.

We show up to work, smiling and nodding like everything's fine, even when we're drowning inside. We become the **"perfect"** partner, saying yes to things we don't want because we're scared of disappointing someone. We laugh at jokes that aren't funny because we want to fit in. And somewhere between all these versions of ourselves the ideal friend, the hardworking employee, the ever-smiling child we forget what it's like to just be ourselves.

The truth is, society trains us from a young age to wear masks. If you've ever been told to **"be polite," "act normal," or *"stop being so emotional,"*** congratulations you've experienced the first nudge to fit in.

But here's the catch: when you wear these masks for too long, you lose sight of who you are underneath. And guess what? The real you is the one the world desperately needs.

• • •

Why Do We Hide Ourselves?

Fear of Rejection

"If they see the real me, they won't love me."

It's a thought that haunts so many of us. The fear of rejection makes us compromise parts of ourselves just to be accepted. But let me tell you something: you are not meant to be liked by everyone. You're not ice cream.

The Pressure to Be Perfect

Perfectionism is the heaviest **mask** we wear. Social media makes it worse. You see someone's highlight reel their perfect vacation, their perfect body, their perfect relationship and suddenly you feel like you're falling behind in life. So, you chase perfection.

But perfection is exhausting. And chasing it only leaves you feeling unworthy when you don't measure up.

The Need to Belong

We humans are wired to connect. But sometimes, in the race to belong, we compromise our authenticity. We say **"yes"** to things we don't want, we laugh when we want to cry, and we silence our voices to avoid standing out.

But let me ask you this: ***what's the point of belonging to a group if you can't belong to yourself?***

The Roles We Play

Let's talk about the roles we're stuck in.

The Perfect Friend: You're always there for others, but when was the last time you were there for yourself?

The Loyal Partner: You lose yourself in a relationship, giving so much love to someone else that you forget to love yourself.

The Overachiever: You measure your worth by how much you get done, but inside, you feel empty and burned out.

Sound familiar? These roles are comforting because they make us feel seen and accepted. But they also keep us trapped.

It's Okay to Step Out of the Role

Here's the truth you need to hear: **it's okay to stop pretending. It's okay to take off the mask and show up as you.**

- If you're tired, say it.
- If you disagree, speak it.
- If you don't want to do something, **don't force yourself to say "yes."**

The people who truly love you will love you for who you are, not who you pretend to be.

A Letter to Your Ideal Self

Let's dig deeper. ***Grab a notebook, a pen, and some honesty.***

Step 1: Write a letter to your ideal self the version of you that you feel you're supposed to be.

What does this **"perfect"** version look like? Is it someone who's always confident, always successful, and never makes mistakes? Write it all down.

Step 2: Now, write about your authentic self the real you. What do you love about yourself? What do you struggle with? What makes you, you?

Step 3: Compare the two letters.

- Which one feels more real?
- Which one feels more freeing?

You'll find that your authentic self might not be perfect, but it's honest. And honesty feels lighter than perfection ever could.

A Quick Reminder

You are not here to live someone else's version of your life. You are not here to please the whole world. You are here to be yourself. And the people who are meant to walk this journey with you will love you exactly as you are **flaws**, **quirks**, and everything in between.

(The world doesn't need another copy. It needs you. Take off the mask. Show up as yourself. And trust that the right people will stay).

"You were born to be real, not perfect."

CHAPTER II

Healing Through Heartbreak

Heartbreak: The One Thing We All Have in Common

Let's start with a fact: at some point in life, we've all felt like our hearts were shattered into a million pieces. first: heartbreak sucks. There's no sugar-coating it. Whether it was a breakup, a betrayal, or just the realization that someone you trusted didn't have your back heartbreak doesn't discriminate. heartbreak feels like someone took a sledgehammer to your chest and walked away without even saying sorry.

It doesn't matter if you're rich, poor, young, or old, Beyoncé or your next-door neighbor. At some point in life, it knocks on everyone's door. Heartbreak is the uninvited guest that shows up at the party, eats all the chips, and leaves you alone to pick up the pieces.

But here's the secret: it's not the end of the world. In fact, it's a part of the human experience. Every one of us has been there, even though it feels like you're the only one in the middle of the ocean of emotions, clinging to a life raft made of tissues and ice cream.

• • •

Let's Talk About the Pain (and Why It's So Weird)

Heartbreak is like a weird mix of physical and emotional pain. Ever noticed how your chest literally hurts after a breakup? That's not just in your head your brain processes emotional pain the same way it processes physical pain. That's why it feels like you've been hit by a truck even though all you did was read their last text: "I think we need to talk..."

And then there's the mental drama. Suddenly, every love song feels like it was written just for you. You start seeing their name everywhere on coffee cups, street signs, even in random cloud shapes. Your brain becomes a chaotic DJ, playing a nonstop loop of memories you wish you could forget.

It's a mess. But guess what? This mess is normal.

The Stages of Grief Yes, It's a Thing

If you've ever wondered why heartbreak feels so chaotic and confusing, it's because it follows a process—a journey, if you will. Think of it as a kind of "emotional road trip." It's long, messy, and the GPS keeps recalculating, but eventually, you'll get there. Let's break it down:

1. Denial

"This can't be happening. They'll text me tomorrow, right? Right?"

You convince yourself it's just a misunderstanding. Maybe they're just busy. Maybe Mercury is in retrograde. (Spoiler alert: it's not Mercury. It's them.)

This is where you're still hoping there's a chance. You text them, even though you swore you wouldn't. You stalk their social media like it's your new job. You tell yourself, "It's fine, they'll come back." The truth is, you're lying to yourself, and deep down, you know it. But hey, denial's a cozy little place. It's like putting your head in the sand and pretending the breakup didn't happen. It's fine. Nothing to see here. Just keep scrolling through their pictures.

2. Anger

"How dare they? After everything I did for them!"
You're suddenly fueled by rage. You fantasize about throwing their favorite hoodie into a bonfire or dramatically returning their things with a "Dear John" OR "Hey Mary" letter.

Here's where the real fun begins. You start thinking about all the things they did wrong. "How could they?" "What was I thinking?" "I should've known better!" It's like a fire has been lit inside you, and suddenly everything is their fault. Their bad habits, their inability to communicate, and oh, don't forget the socks they left on the floor every day. Now, you're angry and you're ready to burn their old hoodie. But please, hold off on that. We don't need to call the fire department.

3. Bargaining

"If I can just get one more chance, I'll do everything differently."
This is when you start negotiating with the universe. You promise to eat healthier, call your mom more, and never binge-watch Netflix again—if only the universe brings them back.

This is when you start thinking, "Okay, maybe I can change. Maybe we can work this out." You make deals with yourself. "I'll stop eating pizza if they come back." Or, "I'll stop wearing sweatpants all day if they just text me one more time." But deep down, you know the truth. You can't bargain with someone's feelings. This is a lesson in acceptance, but not yet. Let's get to the next stage.

4. Depression

"What's the point? I'll never find love again. Might as well adopt 12 cats and call it a day."
The sadness hits like a tidal wave. You start avoiding mirrors, wearing the same sweatpants for a week, and listening to Adele on repeat.

Now we hit the heavy part. You feel like you're sinking into the deepest pit of despair. You can't get out of bed. You don't want to hang out with your friends because, let's be real, they're all happy and in love, and you just want to curl up in a blanket and pretend the world doesn't exist. At this point, you're probably binge-watching sad movies that you know will make you cry but still choose to watch because misery loves company.

The key here: It's okay to feel sad. But remember, this too shall pass. It might take a while, but you will rise from this pit like a majestic phoenix with a glass of wine in hand.

5. Acceptance

"You know what? Maybe this is for the best."
One day, you wake up, and the sun feels a little brighter. You start to see that this heartbreak isn't the end of your story , it's just a plot twist.

Here's the part where you finally say, "Okay, I'm going to be okay." You realize that maybe this breakup wasn't a punishment, but a lesson. It's when you stop checking their social media (finally, thank God). You stop texting them at 2 a.m. with your drunk apologies or emotional outbursts. You come to terms with the fact that life goes on. The world didn't end. You can breathe again. It feels like a big sigh of relief.

• • •

Healing Tools: Let's Get to Work

Now that you're aware of the stages, let's talk about how to heal because trust me, you can't stay stuck in heartbreak forever. It's not healthy, and your future self will thank you for getting off that emotional rollercoaster. Here's what I want you to do:

1. Self-Compassion

Stop being so hard on yourself. Heartbreak hurts, and that's okay. Give yourself permission to feel it. You don't have to rush through the pain. Take time to heal, and be kind to yourself through the process. Heartbreak doesn't mean you're weak, unlovable, or flawed. It just means you're human. Treat yourself the way you'd treat a best friend gentle, kind, and with a lot of ice cream.

2. Acceptance

Accept that it's over.This is the hard part, but it's crucial. Accept that the relationship (or situation) is over. It's not about forgetting them; it's about letting go of the hope that things could've been different.The relationship has ended, and no amount of pleading, bargaining, or emotional manipulation is going to change that. Sometimes, we have to let go of what was to make room for what could be. Think of it as cleaning out your closet—getting rid of the old stuff (old relationships, toxic habits) so there's space for something better to come along.

3. Creating Space for New Beginnings

This part isn't just about getting over someone. It's about getting over yourself—your need for validation, for approval, for someone else to define your worth. It's about rediscovering who you are outside of a relationship. It's about having the courage to believe in new possibilities, even when it feels like you'll never trust again.

So, how do you create space for new beginnings? Start by doing the things that make you feel alive again. Go for a walk, pick up a new hobby, or finally start that book you've been putting off. Fill your life with things that make you happy.

• • •

I know it doesn't feel like it now, but heartbreak comes with a hidden gift: it teaches you about you.

When the dust settles, you'll realize that heartbreak forces you to grow. It makes you reflect on what you want, what you need, and what you absolutely won't tolerate in the future. It teaches you resilience, self-worth, and how to be whole on your own.

What Has Heartbreak Taught You About Your Strength?

Grab your notebook and pour your heart out. Answer these questions:

- What did this heartbreak teach you about your strength?
- What did it reveal about what you truly value in a relationship?
- How can you use this experience to grow and move forward?

It doesn't have to be a perfect answer. Just be real with yourself. Here's why it's important:

Heartbreak can break you down, yes, but it can also build you up. Every time you get through it, you're stronger. You realize that no matter how bad things get, you'll always find a way to stand up again. And that's the real beauty of healing you emerge from it not just as the person you were before, but as someone who can handle whatever life throws your way.

A Quick Reminder

Heartbreak might feel like the end, but it's not. It's a chance to start over, stronger and wiser than before. Remember, the best revenge is living a life so full and joyful that you forget why you were sad in the first place.

The Last Laugh: You'll Be Fine

Here's a little truth bomb for you: You are going to be okay. You will laugh again. You will love again. And when you look back at this moment, you won't see just pain. You'll see the person you became through it all. You'll look back and think, "Wow, I made it through that. I am a badass."

So, give yourself time. Trust the process. And if you ever need a reminder that everything's going to be okay just remember: if Taylor Swift can turn her heartbreak into some of the best music on the planet, you can turn yours into something amazing, too.

"You've survived 100% of your worst days so far. This one is no different."

"Sometimes, the hardest part isn't letting go, but learning to start over." – Nicole Sobon

CHAPTER III

The Power of Forgiving Others (and Yourself)

Forgiveness: *The Heavyweight Champion of Emotional Freedom*

Let's be real forgiveness is one of those things that sounds beautiful in theory but feels impossible in practice. Like, oh sure, I'll just forgive the person who shattered my trust, betrayed me, and ruined my sense of peace no big deal!

Except it is a big deal. And if you've ever held onto resentment for so long that it became part of your personality (*hi, I'm Sarah, and my hobbies include yoga, overthinking, and holding grudges*), you know exactly what I mean.

But here's the thing: forgiveness isn't about the other person. It's about you. Holding onto resentment is like drinking poison and expecting the other person to die. Meanwhile, they're out there living their best life, blissfully unaware that you still rehearse angry monologues in the shower.

So today, we're diving deep into forgiveness not just for others, but for yourself. Because guess what? The person you probably struggle to forgive the most is staring at you in the mirror.

Why Forgiveness is Self-Liberation (and Not a Free Pass for Jerks)

Let's get one thing straight: forgiving someone does NOT mean excusing their behavior. It doesn't mean what they did was okay. It doesn't mean you have to let them back into your life or send them a friendly "Hey, no hard feelings" text (*seriously, don't do that*).

Forgiveness is about freeing yourself. Because the truth is, holding onto resentment and anger takes work. Emotional energy that you could be spending on things that actually make you happy (*like binge-watching your favorite show or learning how to make those fancy coffee drinks at home*).

Think of forgiveness like uninstalling a toxic app on your phone. It's been running in the background, draining your battery, slowing you down. And the moment you delete it? Boom instant relief.

The Steps to Forgive (Without Losing Your Mind in the Process)

So how do you actually forgive someone, especially when they don't deserve it? (*Because let's be honest, some people deserve a strongly worded email from karma*).

Step 1:*Understand the 'Why'*

Ask yourself: Why does this hurt so much? What exactly are you holding onto? Is it the betrayal? The loss of trust? The fact that they never apologized?

Understanding why you're hurt helps you process your emotions instead of just stewing in them.

Step 2: *Accept That You'll Never Get the Apology You Want*

I hate to break it to you, but some people will never say sorry. Either they don't think they did anything wrong, or they genuinely lack the emotional intelligence to understand how they hurt you.

But here's the radical part: you don't need their apology to move on. Closure isn't something they give you it's something you give yourself.

Step 3: *Release the Resentment (Even If It Feels Impossible)*

This one takes time. But every time you catch yourself replaying the hurt, pause and ask: Do I want to keep carrying this? Imagine setting it down like a heavy backpack. Because at some point, you have to decide that your peace is more important than your grudge.

A great trick? Write their name on a piece of paper, scribble all your anger onto it, then rip it up or burn it (safely, please—no accidental arson).

Step 4:*Focus on Growth, Not Revenge*

It's tempting to want karma to handle your enemies while you sit back with popcorn. (We've all dreamed of a dramatic downfall montage for someone who wronged us).

But the real win? Your growth. Living a fulfilling, joyful life is the best "revenge" because it proves that their actions didn't break you.

Now Let's Talk About the Hardest Forgiveness of All Forgiving Yourself

Here's a fun challenge: name one thing you did ten years ago that still makes you cringe.

We're all guilty of something staying in a toxic relationship too long, making a bad decision, hurting someone we love, wearing questionable fashion choices in high school. The problem is, we tend to beat ourselves up over our past mistakes like a broken record.

But let me ask you this: If your best friend made the same mistake, would you keep punishing them for it? Or would you say, "Hey, you were doing the best you could with what you knew at the time"?

Because that's what self-forgiveness is. It's not about pretending you never messed up. It's about recognizing that you've grown since then.

You are not the same person you were when you made those mistakes. Let that sink in.

Actionable Exercise: Write a Forgiveness Letter

Okay, time to do something radical. Grab a pen and paper.

Option 1: Forgive Someone Else

Write a letter to someone who hurt you. You don't have to send it (in fact, please don't if it's just going to start more drama), but write down everything—how they hurt you, how it made you feel, and then, the big one: why you're choosing to let it go.

Option 2: Forgive Yourself

Write a letter to yourself. Apologize for the times you were too hard on yourself. For the mistakes you still hold onto. Then, tell yourself that you are worthy of grace and that you deserve to move forward.

Bonus: Read it out loud to yourself. It's weird at first, but powerful.

A Quick Reminder

Forgiveness doesn't mean forgetting. It doesn't mean making excuses for bad behavior. It means choosing you over resentment. Choosing peace over pain.

Because at the end of the day, you deserve to live unburdened.

"Forgiveness is giving up the hope that the past could have been any different."

— Oprah Winfrey

Understanding Your True - Self

CHAPTER IV

Who Are You Without the Noise? (Understanding - loneliness)

The Fear of Being Alone (*Or, Why Silence Feels So Damn Loud*)

Picture this: You're sitting alone in a quiet room , no phone, no music, no TV. Just you and your thoughts.

How long until you feel the itch to check your notifications? Five minutes? Two? Maybe you don't even make it that far before you start scrolling through Instagram, watching strangers make matcha lattes, and wondering why everyone's life looks more put-together than yours.

We are terrified of silence. We avoid it like it's some horror movie villain. Because the moment we're alone with our thoughts, guess what happens? We actually have to face ourselves.

And that's kind of scary, isn't it?

• • •

Loneliness vs. Solitude: The Great Debate

Most people confuse being alone with being lonely, but they're two completely different things. It's like confusing hunger with boredom just because you feel something doesn't mean you understand what's causing it.

Loneliness, is a craving. It's the aching void that whispers, "You're not enough on your own. You need someone. Anyone." It makes you text your ex at 2 AM (bad idea), say yes to plans you don't even enjoy, or settle for friendships that drain you rather than fulfill you.

Understanding Loneliness

Loneliness is a silent companion that often creeps into our lives when we least expect it. It's that sinking feeling in the pit of our stomachs when we realize we're alone, not just physically, but in the depths of our hearts. But where does this feeling come from? It's not just about being by ourselves; it's about feeling disconnected from others, even when we're surrounded by people.

Loneliness isn't just a passing mood; it's a heavy burden that weighs on our hearts and minds. When we feel lonely, it's like a deep ache that won't go away, a longing for connection and understanding. But when those connections are missing, it can leave us feeling adrift, like ships lost at sea. And this isn't just about feeling sad or isolated; loneliness can have serious consequences for our mental and physical health. It's been linked to depression, anxiety, and even an increased risk of heart disease. So, understanding loneliness isn't just a matter of curiosity; it's a vital step towards protecting our well-being.

In today's world, it might seem paradoxical that loneliness is still such a widespread issue. After all, we're more connected than ever before, thanks to the wonders of technology. We can chat with friends on the other side of the world, share updates with our loved ones in an instant, and scroll through endless feeds of photos and videos. And yet, despite this digital connectivity, many of us still feel lonely. Why? Because while technology can bridge physical distances, it often fails to bridge the emotional gaps between us. We may have hundreds of "friends" online, but how many of them can we truly count on when we need a shoulder to lean on?

The key to understanding loneliness lies in recognizing the difference between quantity and quality when it comes to relationships. It's not about the number of friends we have or the likes on our latest social media post; it's about the depth and authenticity of those connections. Genuine connections are like lifelines that anchor us in times of trouble and lift us up in moments of joy. They're built on trust, empathy, and shared experiences, and they're essential for our emotional well-being. In a world where superficial interactions are the norm, genuine connections are like precious gems waiting to be discovered.

So, why does all this matter? Because loneliness isn't just a personal problem; it's a societal issue with far-reaching consequences. When individuals feel isolated and disconnected, it can erode the fabric of communities and weaken the bonds that hold us together. Loneliness breeds fear, mistrust, and division, creating a vicious cycle of social isolation and alienation. But by understanding the roots of loneliness and the importance of genuine connections, we can begin to break free from this cycle and build a more compassionate and connected world.

Solitude, on the other hand, is a choice. It's the quiet confidence that says, "I'm okay with just me." It's turning off the noise of the world and tuning into yourself. It's realizing that your own company is actually... enjoyable.

Solitude: The Power of Being Alone (*and Actually Enjoying It*)

Solitude is one of the most misunderstood concepts in the world. People hear the word and immediately think of loneliness, sadness, or social failure. But in reality, solitude is a superpower it's where clarity, creativity, and self-awareness thrive.

When you truly embrace solitude, you stop seeing being alone as something to escape from and start seeing it as something to return to. It's not isolation. It's not loneliness. It's a reconnection to yourself, your thoughts, and the things that actually matter.

What Solitude Really Means

Let's clear something up:

- Solitude is not sitting in your room, overthinking everything you've ever said or done.
- Solitude is not binge-watching Netflix alone and calling it "me time."
- Solitude is not loneliness disguised as independence.

Solitude is the deliberate choice to spend time with yourself—not because you have to, but because you want to. It's being alone and feeling full, not empty.

"But I hate being alone."

Of course, you do. Society has conditioned us to fear solitude. Think about it:

- The quiet kid in school? Weird.
- The person eating alone at a restaurant? Pathetic.
- The one who stays in on a Friday night? Must have no friends.

We're taught that if you're alone, something is wrong with you. But that's a lie. Some of the most grounded, successful, and self-assured people in history prioritized solitude.

"I never found the companion that was so companionable as solitude." — Henry David Thoreau

"Solitude is where I place my chaos to rest and awaken my inner peace." — Nikki Rowe

"You cannot be lonely if you like the person you're alone with." — Wayne Dyer

If loneliness is the fear of being alone, solitude is the freedom of being alone.

• • •

Why We Distract Ourselves (And Why It's Making Everything Worse)

Let's be honest: We suck at being alone. The moment we get even a second of stillness, we reach for something our phones, Netflix, a bag of chips, literally anything to avoid being left with our thoughts.

Why?

Because sitting with yourself means confronting things you don't want to think about. The insecurities. The doubts. The things you haven't processed yet.

But here's the thing: avoiding yourself doesn't make the problem go away. It just buries it deeper.

And trust me, buried emotions don't just disappear. They show up in unexpected ways sudden mood swings, unexplained exhaustion, feeling weirdly irritated at people for no reason (*looking at you, Karen from work*).

The only way to understand yourself is to actually spend time with yourself.

How to Disconnect from the Noise and Reconnect with Yourself

Okay, so how do we actually do this? How do we go from "I can't be alone without spiraling" to "Wow, solitude is kind of... nice"?

• • •

Step 1:*Recognize Your Distractions*

What do you reach for when you don't want to be alone? Your phone? Food? Social media? Work? The key isn't to stop completely (**let's be real, no one is quitting their phone cold turkey**), but to notice when you're using distractions to avoid something deeper.

Take Yourself on a Date

Go to a coffee shop. Take a walk. Cook yourself a fancy meal. Do something alone that you'd usually only do with others. It'll feel awkward at first, but soon, you'll realize how peaceful it can be.

Step 2:*Get Comfortable with Silence*

Start small. Five minutes of quiet. Then ten. Then an hour. It's going to feel weird at first, but that's just your brain adjusting.

Try sitting with your thoughts without judgment. Let them come and go like waves. (And no, overthinking every life decision you've ever made doesn't count as productive self-reflection.)

Step 3: Journal Your Feelings (*Yes, Even the Messy Ones*)

Writing forces you to slow down. It helps you see your thoughts instead of just feeling overwhelmed by them.

Grab a notebook and answer these questions:

How do I feel when I'm alone?

What thoughts come up?

What am I avoiding?

What parts of myself do I love? What parts do I struggle with?

Warning: This might get uncomfortable. That's okay. Growth isn't supposed to feel cozy.

One Hour Alone

Here's your challenge: Spend one full hour alone. No phone. No distractions. No music. Just you.

Sounds easy? It's not. But trust me, it'll teach you more about yourself than any self-help book ever could (yes, even this one).

After your hour, journal about the experience. What did you notice? Did you feel restless? Did certain emotions come up? What did you learn?

The Best Relationship You'll Ever Have is with Yourself

At the end of the day, if you can't enjoy your own company, how can you expect anyone else to?

Solitude isn't about isolation—it's about understanding yourself, trusting yourself, and liking yourself. And when you get to that point? That's when life starts to feel a whole lot lighter.

"The quieter you become, the more you can hear."
— Ram Dass

CHAPTER V

Strength in Vulnerability

Vulnerability: The Courage to Be Seen (*Even When It's Terrifying*)

Okay, let's be real nobody wakes up in the morning thinking, *You know what would be fun today? Exposing my deepest fears, emotions, and insecurities to other people!*

Nope.

Vulnerability sounds great in theory, but in reality, it's terrifying. It's like standing in front of an audience in your underwear, hoping no one laughs. It's that moment before you hit "send" on a risky text. It's when you tell someone how you really feel and brace yourself for impact.

And yet, despite all that fear, vulnerability is exactly what makes us human. It's the one thing that has the power to connect us, heal us, and transform us if we're brave enough to embrace it.

But Wait... Isn't Vulnerability a Weakness?

Society has done a fantastic job of convincing us that vulnerability = weakness. We're taught to "be strong," to "never let them see you cry," and to "keep your guard up" because showing emotions somehow makes you fragile.

But here's the truth: Vulnerability isn't weakness, it's bravery in its purest form.

It takes zero courage to hide behind a mask. But opening up? Letting people see the real you? That takes guts. That's the kind of strength that builds deep relationships, real connections, and a life that actually feels fulfilling—not just looks perfect from the outside.

The Real MVPs of Vulnerability (And Why They Inspire Us)

Think about your favorite books, movies, or even real-life people who have moved you. I guarantee their stories weren't built on perfection they were built on struggle.

- Harry Potter wasn't a hero because he was perfect, he was a scrawny, messy-haired kid who admitted he was scared but fought anyway.
- Taylor Swift turned heartbreak and rejection into art that made the whole world feel something (*and yes, we've all cried to one of her songs don't lie*).
- Oprah Winfrey built an empire not because she hid her struggles but because she shared them, her trauma, failures, and comebacks.

The people we admire most aren't the ones who act like they have it all together. They're the ones who show us that even in their brokenness, they are still whole.

And that, my friend, is the power of vulnerability.

How to Start Being Vulnerable (*Without Feeling Like You're Exposing Your Soul on Live TV*)

1.Start Small

You don't have to spill your entire life story in one sitting. Maybe start by admitting when you're having a rough day instead of saying, "I'm fine." (Side note: "I'm fine" is the biggest lie ever told. We all know it.)

2.Find Your Safe People

Not everyone deserves access to your vulnerability. Some people handle it like a fragile treasure. Others? Like a toddler with a chainsaw. Choose wisely.

3.Accept That Not Everyone Will Get It (*And That's Okay*)

Vulnerability isn't about getting a certain response it's about giving yourself permission to be real. Some people won't know how to handle your honesty. That's their problem, not yours.

Embracing Personal Growth Through Adversity

Let's switch gears a little. Because if we're talking about vulnerability, we have to talk about adversity.

Adversity is life's way of slapping us upside the head and saying, "Hey! Are you paying attention? There's a lesson here!"

And even though it sucks in the moment, adversity is one of the greatest teachers you will ever have.

Think about it:

- Every setback has shaped you.
- Every heartbreak has taught you something about love (or at least about what not to tolerate).
- Every failure has given you wisdom, whether you wanted it or not.

So let's stop pretending that struggle is something to be ashamed of. It's actually where the good stuff happens.

Proof That Adversity Builds Strength

1. J.K. Rowling Was Rejected 12 Times Before Publishing Harry Potter

Imagine if she had given up after the 11th rejection. Imagine a world without Hogwarts. (Tragic.)

2. Steve Jobs Was Fired from His Own Company Before Revolutionizing Tech

That's like being kicked out of your own house and then coming back years later to rebuild it into a mansion.

3. Nelson Mandela Spent 27 Years in Prison Before Becoming President

If anyone had a right to be bitter, it was him. Instead, he chose forgiveness. That's next-level resilience.

The point? The strongest people you know weren't born strong. They were shaped by struggle. And so are you.

• • •

Your Struggles = Your Story

If you're in the middle of something hard right now, just know this: One day, this will be part of your story.

The thing that feels impossible now? The heartbreak, the setback, the failure? It won't define you—but it will refine you.

So don't be afraid of being vulnerable. Don't be afraid of adversity.

Because the truth is, your struggles aren't making you weaker. They're making you unstoppable.

• • •

Owning Your Vulnerability

Time to get real. Grab a notebook (*or your Notes app—whatever works*).

1. Write about a time you were truly vulnerable. What happened? How did it feel?
2. Think of a time adversity shaped you for the better. What did you learn?
3. What is one fear about being vulnerable that you want to let go of?

Vulnerability = Strength

At the end of the day, vulnerability isn't about weakness. It's about courage. It's about showing up, even when you're scared. It's about letting yourself be seen.

Because when you allow yourself to be real, you give others permission to do the same. And that? That's how the world changes.

The strongest people are not those who show strength in front of us but those who win battles we know nothing about."

— Jonathan Harnisch

CHAPTER VI

The Voices That Shape Us

Whose Voice Are You Listening To?

If you really stop and think about it, most of the thoughts in your head aren't even yours.

No, seriously. The way you view yourself, the things you believe about success, love, failure most of it has been planted in your mind by someone else. Your family, your friends, your teachers, society, the movies you grew up watching (*yes, even that one Disney film that convinced you love should be effortless*) , they've all shaped the way you think.

Some of those voices have lifted you up. Others? They've clipped your wings before you even had the chance to fly.

So let's talk about them. Because figuring out which voices to keep and which ones to let go of is one of the most important things you'll ever do.

The Voices That Define Us

1. Family: The First Voice You Ever Heard

Before you even knew how to form a thought, your family was shaping how you saw the world. Maybe they told you that success meant a stable job with a good paycheck (because *"log kya kahenge?"*). Maybe they taught you that love should always be selfless (*even when it costs you your own happiness*). Maybe they made you feel like you had to prove your worth before you could be accepted.

But here's the truth: Your family's voice is powerful, but it is not final. You get to decide what to carry forward and what to leave behind.

2. Friends: The Voices We Choose (*or Do We?*)

Ever noticed how we start acting like the people we spend the most time with? It's science. Your brain literally rewires itself based on your closest influences (which explains why you suddenly start using the same phrases as your best friend).

The right friendships will push you to be your best. But the wrong ones? They'll keep you stuck. Be careful who you let into your circle, because their voices will eventually become your own.

3. Society: The Background Noise You Can't Escape

Society is like that one radio station that never stops playing. It tells you what success should look like, how relationships should work, and what kind of life you should be living.

- If you're not married by 30? You're behind.
- If you're not working 24/7? You're lazy.
- If you don't fit the beauty standard? Try harder.

But let's take a moment to acknowledge the ones who broke these so-called rules and changed the game.

The Rebels Who Ignored the Noise

1. Shah Rukh Khan: The Outsider Who Became the King

Before he became King Khan, Shah Rukh Khan was just a guy with a dream. No Bollywood connections. No godfather. Just talent, hard work, and an unshakable belief in himself.

One of his most famous quotes?

"Don't become a philosopher before you become rich."

Translation? Stop overthinking your potential. Do the work, take risks, and make your own destiny.

Imagine if SRK had listened to society telling him, "You don't belong in Bollywood." We wouldn't have *Dilwale Dulhania Le Jayenge*. We wouldn't have *Swades*. We wouldn't have the biggest star India has ever seen.

2. J.K. Rowling: The Woman Who Refused to Quit

Twelve publishers rejected Harry Potter. Twelve. Can you imagine if J.K. Rowling had listened to them? If she had said, "*Maybe they're right. Maybe my story isn't good enough.*"

But she didn't. And now? She built a world that shaped an entire generation.

One of her most famous quotes?

"Rock bottom became the solid foundation on which I rebuilt my life."

What does that teach us? That failure isn't a full stop. It's a comma.

3. Steve Jobs: The Guy Who Got Fired From His Own Company

Imagine creating something, only to be told, "Yeah, thanks, but we don't need you anymore." That's exactly what happened to Steve Jobs when he was kicked out of Apple.

But instead of giving up, he built something better. And when he came back to Apple years later, he turned it into the tech giant we know today.

His lesson?

"Your time is limited, so don't waste it living someone else's life."

Which Voices Should You Keep?

Now, let's get personal. It's time to sort through the voices in your head and decide which ones are helping you and which ones are holding you back.

Ask yourself:

1.Does this voice push me forward or pull me back?

If it motivates you, keep it. If it drains you, it's time to let it go.

2.Does this voice belong to someone who truly knows me?

Your parents, teachers, and bosses may mean well, but that doesn't mean they know what's best for you.

3.Would I say these things to a friend?

If the voice in your head is cruel, critical, and unforgiving—replace it with one that speaks to you with kindness.

Whose Voices Shaped You?

Take out a notebook and reflect on this:

- Write about the most influential voices in your life.
- Which ones helped you grow?
- Which ones made you doubt yourself?
- What's one voice you need to let go of today?

Your Voice is the One That Matters Most

At the end of the day, the loudest voice in your life should be yours. Not your parents'. Not society's. Not that one judgmental relative who keeps asking when you're getting married.

So here's the challenge: Drown out the noise. Trust your gut. And write your own damn story.

"Don't let the noise of others' opinions drown out your own inner voice."

— Steve Jobs

Living Fully

CHAPTER VII

Turning Struggles Into Stories (A Love Letter to Procrastinators, Overthinkers, and the Chronically Unmotivated)

Raise your hand if you've ever looked at successful peo

Let's be real for a second. If there were a global competition for putting things off until the last minute, most of us would have gold medals by now. If procrastination were an Olympic sport, we'd all be national heroes.

I mean, have you ever noticed how you suddenly have urgent things to do when a deadline is creeping up? You have a report due tomorrow? Perfect time to clean your entire room, research the life expectancy of jellyfish, and stare at the ceiling wondering where it all went wrong.

Or, my personal favorite: deciding to finally start something important... but only after watching just one more YouTube video, which somehow turns into a three-hour deep dive into conspiracy theories about the moon landing.

If this sounds like you, congratulations—you are officially a member of the Procrastinators Club™, where the motto is ***"I'll do it later."***

And guess what? You're not alone.

The Lies We Tell Ourselves About Success

ple and thought:
"Wow, they must have it all figured out. They probably wake up at 5 AM, drink green smoothies, meditate for an hour, and never binge-watch Netflix until 3 AM."

Now, put your hand down because that's a complete myth.

Here's the truth: Every successful person you admire has failed. Repeatedly. Spectacularly.

J.K. Rowling was rejected 12 times.
Steve Jobs got fired from his own company.
Shah Rukh Khan was told he had no future in Bollywood.

They all had struggles. They all faced rejection. But instead of letting those failures define them, they turned their setbacks into stories ones of resilience, growth, and, ultimately, success.

And guess what? So can you.

But first, we need to talk about the three biggest villains in your story: procrastination, laziness, and self-doubt.

Procrastination: *The Art of Doing Everything Except the One Thing You Need to Do*

Let's talk about why we procrastinate because it's not just about being "lazy." In fact, procrastination has nothing to do with laziness. If anything, we procrastinators work twice as hard just in the wrong direction.

Why do we do it?

Fear of Failure – If you don't start, you can't fail. Simple logic, right? Except that's like refusing to take a driving test because you might fail so instead, you never learn to drive at all.

Perfectionism – We convince ourselves that if we're not going to do something perfectly, we shouldn't do it at all. But spoiler alert: perfection doesn't exist. You're better off starting messy than never starting at all.

Overwhelm Paralysis – The task feels too big, too impossible, too much. So instead of doing some of it, we do none of it and stress about it for days. (*Which, ironically, is way more exhausting than just doing the thing.*)

Sound familiar? Thought so.

But here's the worst part: procrastination doesn't just delay our work it delays our dreams. We put off writing that book, starting that business, hitting the gym, learning a new skill, because we think we have time.

Until one day, we look back and realize time moved forward, but we didn't.

Laziness: *The Lie We Tell Ourselves*

Raise your hand if you've ever called yourself lazy.

Now put it down, because you're not lazy.

No, really.

The problem isn't that you're unmotivated or that you "just don't have the energy." It's that you haven't figured out how to light your own fire.

Think about it.

- You can't focus on work, but you have no problem focusing on a 10-episode Netflix binge.
- You don't feel like doing your assignments, but you suddenly have all the energy in the world for scrolling social media for three hours straight.

See? It's not laziness—it's interest.

We're not lazy. We're just bored. Or uninspired. Or, let's be honest, a little scared of what happens if we actually try and things don't go the way we want.

But here's the truth: Waiting for motivation to strike is like waiting for a cat to do what you tell it to. It's just not going to happen.

You don't find motivation. You create it.

How? By starting. Even when you don't feel like it. Especially when you don't feel like it. Because action breeds momentum, and momentum makes things easier.

Self-Doubt: *The Voice That Holds You Back*

Let's talk about the inner critic—you know, that annoying little voice in your head that loves to tell you:

- "You're not good enough."
- "You'll never succeed."
- "Why even try?"

If self-doubt were a person, I'd file a restraining order.

And yet, we listen to it. We believe it. We let it control our lives.

But here's the truth: Self-doubt is just fear wearing a fake mustache.

- Fear of looking stupid.
- Fear of failing.
- Fear of people judging us.

But do you know what happens if you keep waiting until you "feel ready" or "feel confident enough" to do something?

Nothing.

Because confidence isn't what you start with—it's what you earn after you do the scary thing.

The only way to beat self-doubt is to prove it wrong.

How to Turn Struggles into Strengths

Alright, we've talked about the problem. Now let's fix it.

Step 1: Reframe Your Struggle

Instead of saying:

- "I'm lazy." → Say: "I just haven't found what excites me yet."
- "I suck at this." → Say: "I'm still learning."
- "I'm a failure." → Say: "I'm in progress."

The words you use shape your reality. Choose better ones.

Step 2: Start Before You Feel Ready

If you wait until you feel like doing something, you'll never do it. The secret? Start anyway.

- Want to write a book? Write a bad first page.
- Want to get fit? Do one push-up.
- Want to start a business? Launch before you overthink it.

Step 3: Rewrite Your Narrative

Time for an exercise. Think of a failure, setback, or struggle you've been through. Now, write about it in two ways:

- The Victim Version – Write about how it ruined you, how unfair it was, how much it sucked.
- The Hero Version – Write about how it shaped you, what it taught you, and how it made you stronger.

The story you tell yourself defines your future. Choose wisely.

You Are Not Behind

If you've ever felt like you've "wasted time" because of procrastination, laziness, or fear, listen up:

You are not late. You are exactly where you need to be.

You are not running behind some imaginary timeline. Life is not a race. You are still becoming who you're meant to be.

And that means you can start today. Right now. No more waiting. No more "I'll do it later." No more listening to the voice that tells you you're not good enough.

You are good enough. You always have been.

Now go prove it.

"Doubt kills more dreams than failure ever will." *— Suzy Kassem*

CHAPTER VIII

FOMO : The Generation of Fear – Chasing Everything, Finding Nothing

Let's talk about fear.

Not the fear of ghosts, heights, or horror movies. Not the fear of spiders (*even though, let's be real, those things are terrifying*). I'm talking about the fear that has infected an entire generation—the fear of missing out.

Missing out on love.

Missing out on success.

Missing out on looking perfect, having the perfect relationship, living the perfect life.

And this fear? It's everywhere. It's in the way we obsessively scroll through social media, convincing ourselves that everyone else has their life together. It's in the way we chase relationships, validation, and the illusion of happiness because if we're not doing what everyone else is doing, then we must be failing, right?

Wrong.

Because in the pursuit of everything, we are losing ourselves.

The Fear of Missing Out: *The Silent Epidemic*

Let's be honest. This generation is tired. And I don't mean the "I need more sleep" kind of tired (*although, yeah, that too*). I mean mentally exhausted. Because no matter what we do, it never feels like enough.

Why? Because we live in a world that constantly tells us:

- "If you're single, you're failing at love."
- "If you're not rich by 25, you're doing life wrong."
- "If you're not constantly happy, something is missing."

And so we chase everything relationships, money, status, approval thinking that somewhere in this endless pursuit, we'll finally feel whole.

But let's talk about what's really happening.

Chasing Relationships vs. Self-Destruction

The Illusion of "The Perfect Relationship"

Social media has convinced us that if our love life isn't cinematic, something must be wrong. Couples post highlight reels of their relationships, making it seem effortless but real love is messy, hard, and takes actual work.

And yet, so many people in this generation:

- Stay in toxic relationships because they're afraid of being alone.
- Settle for less than they deserve just to say they have someone.
- Jump from person to person, never actually healing just distracting themselves.

It's not love we're chasing. It's the fear of being unchosen.

Hookup Culture: The Fast Food of Love

Now, let's talk about the other extreme: the "I don't catch feelings" mindset.

The culture of casual hookups, situationships, and "we don't label things" has made relationships feel disposable. Love isn't about connection anymore it's about convenience.

- Swipe right.
- Have a meaningless conversation.
- Meet up.
- Ghost them when it gets too real.

This generation is **terrified of commitment** because commitment means vulnerability. And vulnerability? That's too risky.

But here's the catch **no one wins in this game.** Because while we tell ourselves we don't care, deep down, we do.

We were never meant to love like this halfway, out of fear, with one foot already out the door.

The Cult of External Validation

Let's switch gears for a second. Because it's not just relationships we're chasing it's approval.

Think about it.

How much of what you do is for you and how much is for the image of you?

- The picture-perfect Instagram post.
- The luxury brands, even when your bank account is crying.
- The pressure **to be liked, be admired, be seen as "successful."**

But here's what no one tells you: **External validation is a black hole.**

No matter how much approval you get, it will never be enough. Because there will always be someone doing more. Someone prettier, richer, more successful, more loved.

And if you live your life chasing them, you will never live for yourself.

Boys vs. Girls: How This Generation is Breaking Itself

Let's get real about something.

Men and women are not dealing with the same struggles but both are suffering.

What Women Are Going Through:

- **Unrealistic beauty standards** – If you're not curvy, you need surgery. If you have curves, they better be in the "right" places.
- **Emotional exhaustion** – Expected to be strong but also "soft." Independent but not "too much."
- **Romantic pressure** – If you're single, something must be wrong with you. If you're married, you should be balancing a perfect career and a perfect home.

Women today are expected to be everything at once and it's crushing them.

• • •

What Men Are Going Through:

- **Emotional suppression** – Told to "man up" instead of express how they feel.
- **Career pressure** – If you're not rich and successful by 30, are you even a "real man"?
- **The fear of not being enough** – Not tall enough, not strong enough, not successful enough.

Men are **suffering in silence** because society has made them believe that asking for help makes them weak.

The truth? **Both genders are drowning**. Just in different ways.

The Road Back to Ourselves

Alright. We've talked about the problem. Let's talk about the solution.

1. Stop Living for the Camera

If social media didn't exist, what would you actually want? If no one could see your life, who would you be?

Live for you, not for their likes.

2. Stop Searching for Yourself in Other People

If you don't know who you are alone, you won't know who you are with someone else. Get to know yourself first.

3. Understand That External Validation is an Addiction

The more you chase it, the emptier you'll feel. Real happiness comes from within cliché but true.

4. Let Go of the "Timeline"

You are not behind in life. The pressure to have everything figured out by 25? It's a scam. Move at your own pace.

5. Choose Real Over Perfect

In relationships, in success, in happiness chase what's real, not what looks good.

You Are Not Missing Out

If you've ever felt like you're falling behind in life you're not.

If you've ever felt like you're not "good enough" because society told you so you are.

This generation is so busy chasing everything, we're forgetting what really matters.

But here's the truth: You are not missing out on anything when you are busy building yourself.

Let them chase. Let them run in circles. You? You focus on becoming.

Because that's the only thing that lasts.

"What if the thing you're missing out on... is the life you're meant to build?"

CHAPTER IX

The Symphony of Balance – When Life Feels Like a Juggling Act

Ever feel like you're trying to do everything at once be a great friend, build a successful career, stay in shape, eat healthy, get enough sleep, have an active social life, work on your passions, and maybe, just maybe, find time to breathe?

Yeah, me too.

It's like juggling flaming swords while riding a unicycle. One wrong move and boom you're on fire, wondering why you even tried in the first place.

Society tells us we can "have it all." That we should be grinding 24/7, maintaining the perfect social life, working out daily, having a thriving romantic relationship, all while remaining calm and unbothered.

Reality check? That's a scam.

Balance isn't about doing everything perfectly. It's about doing what matters most without losing yourself in the process.

Let's talk about it.

Why Balance Feels Impossible

If balance feels like a myth to you, it's probably because you're trying to give 100% to everything at the same time.

The problem? That's **mathematically impossible.**

You can't be fully present in your career and fully present in your relationships and fully present in your self-care at the same time. Something will always require more attention than the other.

So instead of trying to "balance" like it's a perfect equation, think of life like a symphony.

The Symphony of Balance

In an orchestra, different instruments take the lead at different times. Sometimes the violins are front and center, sometimes it's the piano, sometimes the drums. But they all come together to create harmony.

Life works the same way.

- Some weeks, your career takes the lead.
- Some weeks, your relationships need more attention.
- Some weeks, your mental health is the priority.

And that's okay. The key isn't to divide your energy equally—it's to give the right amount of energy to the right thing at the right time.

The Three Pillars: Relationships, Career, and Self-Care

Let's break this down. Because if balance is a symphony, these are your main instruments.

1. Relationships: The Heartbeat of Life

At the end of the day, **relationships are what make life meaningful**. But in a world that glorifies "**hustle culture,**" it's easy to put them on the back burner.

Raise your hand if you've ever:

- Canceled plans because you were "too busy" (*but really, you just wanted to scroll on your phone in peace*).
- Taken someone for granted because *"they'll always be there."*
- Let work stress turn you into a **walking thunderstorm** around your loved ones.

We all have.

Here's the thing: **Success means nothing if you have no one to share it with.**

So while chasing your dreams, don't forget to:

✓ Call your parents.

✓ Be present with your friends.

✓ Make time for love-real love, not just "convenient love."

Because at the end of the day, **relationships are what make us human.**

2. Career: The Hustle Trap vs. The Meaningful Work

Now let's talk about the thing that keeps most of us up at night our careers.

Some of us are **obsessed with work,** convinced that *if we don't grind every second, we'll fall behind.* Others feel **stuck and directionless,** wondering if we'll ever find a job that actually makes us happy.

The truth? Both extremes are exhausting.

✓ If you're overworking yourself, remember: **Money can be made again. Time cannot.**

✓ If you're lost in your career, remember: **No one has it figured out. Keep moving. It'll come together.**

Work hard, but **don't lose yourself** to the hustle. Because at the end of your life, no one's going to remember how many emails you answered. They'll remember the person you were.

3. Self-Care: The Most Neglected Priority

How often do we prioritize ourselves last?

- "I'll sleep when I'm successful."
- "I don't have time to relax I have things to do."
- "Self-care is selfish." (It's not.)

Listen up: You cannot pour from an empty cup. If you burn yourself out trying to be everything for everyone, you'll wake up one day completely drained, wondering where you went.

Self-care isn't a luxury it's a necessity.

✔ Rest when you need to.

✔ Take breaks without guilt.

✔ Set boundaries that protect your peace.

Your well-being is **not negotiable.**

How to Prioritize What Matters Most

Alright, let's make this practical. How do you actually find balance without feeling like you're constantly failing at something?

Step 1: The Priority Pyramid

Imagine a pyramid with three levels:

1. **The Foundation (Non-Negotiables)** – The things that keep you grounded (health, relationships, mental peace).
2. **The Middle (Important but Flexible)** – Career growth, social life, personal projects.
3. **The Top (Extras)** – Hobbies, entertainment, social media (aka, the stuff that drains your time if you let it).

Now, ask yourself: **Am I spending too much energy on the top of the pyramid and not enough on the foundation?**

If so, it's time to **rearrange your priorities.**

Step 2: The "Hell Yes or No" Rule

If something isn't a **"HELL YES,"** it should probably be a no.

Life is too short to fill with half-hearted commitments and energy-draining obligations. Protect your time like it's your most valuable currency because it is.

Step 3: Accept That Balance Looks Different Every Day

Some days, balance looks like:

✔ Finishing all your work, eating healthy, and getting 8 hours of sleep.

Other days, balance looks like:

✔ Eating instant noodles at midnight while rewatching your favorite show because you just need a break.

And guess what? **Both are okay.**

Balance isn't about **perfection** it's about **awareness.**

Balance is Not a Destination—It's a Daily Choice

Here's the truth: **There will never be a perfect balance between relationships, career, and self-care.**

Some days, work will demand more.
Some days, your relationships will need extra love.
Some days, you will need to pause and recharge.

And that's okay. The key is to **adjust, realign, and keep moving forward.**

Because life isn't about getting it **perfectly right** it's about learning to dance with the chaos and still finding your rhythm.

"Balance is not something you find. It's something you create."

— Jana Kingsford

CHAPTER X

The Art of Staying Present – How to Stop Living in Fast-Forward

Let's be honest. Most of us aren't really living in the present.

We're either stuck in **replay mode**, obsessing over past mistakes, heartbreaks, and that one embarrassing thing we said in 2016... or we're in **fast-forward mode**, constantly worrying about the future our careers, relationships, bank accounts, or whether AI is eventually going to replace us all.

Meanwhile, the present?

The actual life we're supposed to be living?

It's slipping through our fingers.

We scroll mindlessly.

We rush through meals without tasting them.

We spend time with loved ones while half-listening, half-texting someone else.

And we wonder why life feels so exhausting.

But here's the truth: **Peace is not found** in the past. It's not waiting in the future. It's only ever available in the now.

So let's talk about it 'the art of being here, now, and fully alive.

Why We Struggle to Be Present

Ever noticed how kids experience life? How they get excited about everything—bugs, puddles, the way light reflects off a window?

Somewhere along the way, we lost that.

Because as we grow up, the world teaches us to constantly chase the next thing.

- **As kids?** "Just wait until you're a teenager then life gets fun!"
- **As teenagers?** "College is where it's at! Just get through high school."
- **As adults?** "Find a good job, settle down, and THEN you'll be happy."

And when we get there? We realize the next milestone didn't magically fix everything. So we keep chasing, keep searching never fully arriving.

But happiness doesn't live in "someday." It lives in this **exact moment.**

The problem? **We're too distracted to notice it.**

The Three Biggest Distractions That Steal the Present

1. The Endless Scroll (AKA, The Black Hole of Social Media)

How many times have you picked up your phone for "just a second," only to look up an hour later, wondering where the time went?

Social media is designed to keep you hooked. The dopamine hit of likes, comments, and mindless scrolling **tricks your brain into thinking you're engaged when in reality, you're just zoning out.**

And meanwhile?

The sun sets outside your window.

Your family is talking in the next room.
Life is happening.
And you missed it.

2. The Obsession with "What's Next?"

We live in a **productivity-obsessed** world that convinces us that if we're not planning our next move, we're falling behind.

- Already thinking about the next vacation before the current one ends.
- Stressing about Monday while it's still Saturday night.
- Constantly feeling like where we are isn't enough.

The result? **We never truly arrive anywhere.**

3. The Weight of the Past

Let's not forget about the past. Oh, the past.

We replay our worst moments like a broken record, beating ourselves up for things we cannot change.

- That relationship we messed up.
- That opportunity we didn't take.
- That time we embarrassed ourselves at a party (*and everyone probably forgot about it except us*).

But holding onto the past only steals the present. It's like trying to drive forward while staring in the rearview mirror you're going to crash.

How to Actually Stay Present (*Without Moving to the Himalayas and Becoming a Monk*)

You don't need to give up your phone or meditate for five hours a day to be more present. You just need to make a few **small, intentional shifts** in your daily life.

1. The 5-4-3-2-1 Grounding Technique

Feeling overwhelmed? Caught in your thoughts? Use this trick:

- **5 things you can see** (the color of the sky, the way the light hits your desk, your reflection in the window).
- **4 things you can touch** (your clothes, the ground beneath you, the texture of your hands).
- **3 things you can hear** (birds outside, the hum of a fan, your own breathing).
- **2 things you can smell** (coffee, perfume, fresh air).
- **1 thing you can taste** (mint gum, tea, toothpaste).

This simple exercise instantly brings you back to the present.

2. Eat Like You Actually Care

When was the last time you *really tasted your food?* Like, actually sat down and noticed the flavors, textures, and smells without scrolling through your phone?

- Try this:
- Take a bite.
- Chew slowly.

Notice everything about it—the taste, the temperature, how it feels.

This is **mindful eating**. It turns something as simple as a meal into an experience.

3. The "Phone-Free" Hour

Every day, dedicate **at least one hour** to being completely screen-free. No notifications, no scrolling just existing.

- Go for a walk.
- Read a book.
- Sit in silence (*yes, silence it won't kill you*).

You'd be amazed at how much more alive you feel when you stop checking out of the moment.

4. The "Pause and Breathe" Rule

Before rushing into the next task, pause.

- Breathe in for four seconds.
- Hold for four seconds.
- Breathe out for four seconds.

This tiny act resets your nervous system and brings you **back to now.**

• • •

A 10-Minute Mindfulness Exercise

Step 1: Sit Somewhere Quiet

Find a space with no distractions. It could be your room, a park, or even your car.

Step 2: Close Your Eyes and Focus on Your Breathing

Feel the air filling your lungs. Feel your body relax.

Step 3: Tune Into Your Senses

- What do you hear?
- What do you feel?
- What do you smell?

Step 4: Notice Your Thoughts—But Don't Chase Them

Your mind will wander. That's okay. Just notice your thoughts and let them float by—like clouds in the sky.

Step 5: Open Your Eyes and Carry That Awareness With You

Congratulations. You just practiced mindfulness.

Life is Happening Right Now

If you take one thing from this chapter, let it be this:

You are never going to be younger than you are right now.
You will never get this exact moment again.

So put down your phone.
Take a deep breath.
And be here.

Because this , this is life.

"Realize deeply that the present moment is all you ever have. Make the NOW the primary focus of your life." *— Eckhart Tolle*

CHAPTER XI

Creating Your Legacy

What If You're Remembered for More Than Just Existing?

Let's cut straight to it.

One day, your name will be spoken for the last time. Your social media accounts will turn into ***digital graveyards.*** The world will move forward.

That's not meant to be depressing it's meant to be real.

The question is: **When you're gone, what will you have left behind?**

- Will you be remembered for the way you made people feel?
- For the stories you told?
- For the kindness you gave, the risks you took, the dreams you chased?

Or will you be forgotten because you spent your entire life just existing blending in, doing what was expected, waiting for the "right time" to finally start living?

Here's the thing: **You don't have to be famous to leave a legacy**. You don't have to build an empire, write bestsellers, or have a statue in your honor.

Legacy isn't about how many people remember your name it's about how you impact the people who do.

So let's talk about it.

What Does Legacy Really Mean?

When people think about legacy, they imagine big things historical figures, inventors, billionaires. But legacy isn't just about what you do it's about who you are.

It's about the conversations that change someone's perspective.

It's about the little moments of kindness that people never forget.

It's about the way you showed up fully, authentically, fearlessly.

Your legacy isn't waiting for you in the future. You are writing it right now.

The question is: **Are you writing a story worth remembering?**

The Lies We Believe About Legacy

Let's address the three biggest myths people believe about leaving a legacy.

1. "I Need to Be Someone Important First."

No, you don't.

Some of the most **impactful people** in history weren't rich, powerful, or famous. They were teachers, artists, friends, parents people who changed the world in quiet, everyday ways.

If you've ever **inspired someone, helped someone, made someone's day better,** you've already started leaving a legacy.

2. *"I Have Plenty of Time to Figure It Out."*

Do you?

Because most people wake up one day **realizing they spent years waiting** ,waiting for the perfect moment, the right opportunity, the "*someday*" that never came.

Legacy isn't something you "start working on" in your 50s.

It's being built right now in the choices you make daily.

3. *"I Don't Have Anything Special to Offer."*

Biggest. Lie. Ever.

You don't need to change the entire world.

But you can change someone's world.

- A book that helps someone feel understood.
- A kind word that someone carries forever.
- A small act of courage that inspires someone else to be brave.

The world doesn't need another **"perfect"** person.

It **needs you** raw, real, and willing to show up as yourself.

How to Live a Life That Actually Means Something

1. *Define What Matters Most to You*

If everything was stripped away—money, status, achievements—what would still matter to you?

Because that is the foundation of your legacy.

Ask yourself:

✔ What do I want to be known for?

✔ What impact do I want to have on the people around me?

✔ What values do I want to stand for—no matter what?

Your **legacy isn't a goal**. It's a way of living.

2. Start Living Authentically (No More Pretending)

The most unforgettable people aren't the ones who try to be liked by everyone.

They're the ones who are fully, **unapologetically themselves.**

So stop worrying about:

- Whether people approve of your choices.
- Whether you're "successful enough" by society's standards.
- Whether you fit the mold that was never meant for you in the first place.

Live **boldly**. Live **honestly**. Live in a way that makes you proud of the story you're writing.

3. Give More Than You Take

No, this isn't about donating money (though if you can, cool).

It's about giving in ways that **actually matter:**

✔ Give time to the people who love you.

✔ Give encouragement to those who need it.

✔ Give kindness, even when the world feels cruel.

Your legacy isn't what you get it's what you **leave behind in others.**

Write a Letter to Your Future Self

It's time to get personal.

Grab a notebook (*or open your notes app*, if that's more your style).

Write a letter to **your future self,** answering these questions:

1. What do I want to be remembered for?
2. If I died tomorrow, what would I regret not doing?
3. What kind of person do I want to be 10 years from now?
4. Am I living in a way that aligns with the legacy I want to leave?

Seal it. Save it. Read it in a year.

And if you don't like the answer? **Change your story**

Your Legacy Begins Now

One day, your time will run out. That's just the truth.

But between now and then?

You have a choice.

To live with purpose.

To love fully.

To leave behind something real.

The question isn't whether you'll leave a legacy.

The question is **what kind of legacy you'll leave.**

So start today.

Start now.

And make it one worth remembering.

"Carve your name on hearts, not tombstones. A legacy is etched into the lives we touch, not the things we leave behind."

— Shannon L. Alder

The Art Of Being You

The Art of Being You

Being yourself in a world that profits off your self-doubt is an act of rebellion.

It's about unlearning the rules that were never meant for you.

It's about healing, forgiving, and showing up for yourself.

It's about giving yourself permission to take up space, even when the world tells you to shrink.

This book? It's not here to fix you because you were never broken to begin with.

It's here to help you rediscover who you are underneath all the noise.

It's here to remind you that your struggles your loneliness, your heartbreak, your self-doubt don't define you.

It's here to show you that your worth isn't found in the approval of others, but in the way you choose to love and accept yourself.

And if you've ever felt like you're too much, not enough, or somehow both at the same time?

Welcome. You're exactly where you need to be.

By the time you finish this book, my hope is that you'll stop searching for the right way to be and **start embracing the realest, rawest, most unfiltered version of yourself.**

Because the greatest thing you'll ever do?

Is learn to be **unapologetically you.**

"You owe it to yourself to be the most honest version of you."

About The Author

Arpit Sadh *is an author, designer, and storyteller who has been shaping ideas and narratives since 2011, He's Rooted in spiritualism and a deep love for human connection, he believes in the power of words ,his "wordlings" to inspire, engage, and leave a lasting impact. His mission is simple: to be a presence people can connect with, a storyteller who sparks thought, and a voice that resonates beyond the pages.*

Connect: On Instagram , Linkdln , Medium.
@thearpitsadh (author)

www.ingramcontent.com/pod-product-compliance
Lightning Source LLC
Chambersburg PA
CBHW051057130726
48008CB00008B/33

9798897241729